Evelyn Und

CW00435608

☐ CHRISTIAN SPIRITUALITY SERIES ☐

Evelyn Underhill
on Prayer

Compiled and edited

by

Tony Castle

Marshall Pickering

Marshall Morgan and Scott
Marshall Pickering
34 – 42 Cleveland Street
London W1P 5FB

Copyright © 1989 Tony Castle

First published in 1989 by Marshall Morgan and Scott Publications Ltd
Part of the Marshall Pickering Holdings Group

All rights reserved. No part of this publication may be reproduced, stored
in a retrieval system, or transmitted, in any form or by any means,
electronic, mechanical, photocopying, recording or otherwise, without the
prior permission in writing, of the publisher

British Library CIP Data

Underhill, Evelyn, *1875-1941*
    Evelyn Underhill on Prayer
    1. Christian life. Prayer
    I. Title II. Castle, Tony, *1938-*
    III. Series
    248.3′2

ISBN 0-551-01767-8

Text Set in Baskerville by Avocet Robinson, Buckingham
Printed in Great Britain by Henry Ling Ltd., at the Dorset Press,
Dorchester, Dorset

Contents

Introduction

How I wish that I had discovered Evelyn Underhill's writings when I was a student! Then I was hungry to know more about meditation, mysticism and the life of the Spirit, but sadly her books were not available in our college library. I managed with other more obscure writers but all the while Evelyn's work was really answering the questions that I was posing.

No English woman this century has done more to disentangle misconceptions, clarify and popularise a wider understanding and appreciation of genuine Christian Spirituality and Mysticism. In the 1920s and 1930s by her writing (over twenty books on contemplation and meditation), her radio talks, retreats and conferences she became the acknowledged authority on the Spiritual Life.

Although Evelyn still has admirers and followers little of her work is now available. This little collection is offered by way of an introduction and a reminder of her contribution to the Anglican tradition.

Biographical Note

Evelyn Underhill was a wonderful example and advertisement for the Christian Faith. An intellectual of great spiritual depth she was also a vivid personality with a keen sense of humour and a great love of the outdoor life. Like her father, and her husband, she had a passionate interest in yachting and her pastime pursuits included such diverse things as bookbinding and the love of pets.

The only child of Sir Arthur and Lady Alice Underhill, her youth was passed surrounded by the trappings of the Law, (her father was a distinguished London barrister). She started writing at sixteen and her first published work was a collection of humorous poems entitled *A Bar-Lamb's Ballad Book*. Evelyn was educated at home and went to King's College, London. Every Spring she travelled widely on the Continent and was attracted to the Roman Catholicism that she encountered on her travels. The condemnation of Modernism by the Roman Catholic Church put her off and when she was converted to Christianity she joined the High Church of the Church of England. In 1907, the year of her conversion, she married Hubert Stuart Moore, a barrister whom she had known from childhood. (They had no children.)

In her long and deep spiritual struggles Evelyn had discovered the writings of the great Christian mystics, both Catholic and Protestant. This discovery which, with her conversion, had brought her peace and fulfilment, now became a totally absorbing interest. Finding no comprehensive guide to Christian mysticism she set out to remedy this and her research gave birth to the acclaimed study *Mysticism*, published in 1911. That same year she came under the influence of the Roman Catholic spiritual writer, Baron Friedrich von Hügel, who remained her spiritual guide and mentor until his death in 1925.

In addition to her many articles, books and talks on prayer, contemplation and mysticism Evelyn translated, for the ordinary reader, many of the great classical works of the mystics, for example, *The Cloud of Unknowing* (1912) and *The Scale of Perfection* (1923). In 1924 she began to conduct retreats and conferences on the spiritual life. This was the beginning of a ministry which extended the rest of her life, until she became the most sought after speaker and spiritual guide in the United Kingdom.

Evelyn loved to quote St Teresa of Avila's saying, 'To give Our Lord a perfect service Martha and Mary must combine.' This she took to heart and her mornings were devoted to writing, while in the afternoons she would go out to visit the sick and the poor. Slowly spiritual direction, which was occasional in the afternoon, grew until it occupied nearly the whole day.

Her 'wholeness' of personality and approach to spiritual matters made her a very attractive person, greatly loved and admired by countless people. Evelyn's powerful driving force was a passionate desire to help people find the Christ that she had found and guide them in their developing relationship with him. For this reason she would be delighted that this very small and limited sample of her work is now made available.

The House of Prayer

Temple or Castle

When St Paul described our mysterious human nature as a 'Temple of the Holy Spirit – a created dwelling-place or sanctuary of the uncreated and invisible Divine Life' – he was stating in the strongest possible terms a view of our status, our relation to God, which has always been present in Christianity; and is indeed implicit in the Christian view of Reality. But that statement as it stands seems far too strong for most of us. We do not feel in the very least like the temples of Creative Love. We are more at ease with St Teresa, when she describes the soul as an 'interior castle' a roomy mansion, with various floors and apartments from the basement upwards; not all devoted to exalted uses, not always in a satisfactory state. And when, in a more homely mood, she speaks of her own spiritual life as 'becoming solid like a house', we at last get something we can grasp.

The House of the Soul

The soul's house, that interior dwelling-place which we all possess, for the upkeep of which we are responsible – a place in which we can meet God, or from which in a sense we can exclude God – that is not too big an idea for us. Though no imagery drawn from the life of sense can ever be adequate to the strange and delicate contacts, tensions, demands and benedictions of the life that lies beyond sense: though the important part of every

10

parable is that which it fails to express: still, here is a conception which can be made to cover many of the truths that govern the interior life of prayer.

First, we are led to consider the position of the house. However interesting and important its peculiarities may seem to the tenant, it is not as a matter of fact an unusually picturesque and interesting mansion made to an original design, and set in its own grounds with no other building in sight. Christian spirituality knows nothing of this sort of individualism. It insists that we do not inhabit detached residences, but are parts of a vast spiritual organism; that even the most hidden life is never lived for itself alone. Our soul's house forms part of the vast City of God. Though it may not be an important mansion with a frontage on the main street, nevertheless it shares all the obligations and advantages belonging to the city as a whole. It gets its water from the mains, and its light from the general supply. The way we maintain and use it must have reference to our civic responsibilities.

Part of the City

It is true that God creates souls in a marvellous liberty and variety. The ideals of the building estate tell us nothing about the Kingdom of Heaven. It is true also, that the furnishing of our rooms and cultivation of our garden is largely left to our personal industry and good taste. Still, in a general way, we must fall in with the city's plan; and consider, when we hang some new and startling curtains, how they will look from the street. However intense the personal life of each soul may be, that personal life has got out of proportion, if it makes us forget our municipal obligations and advantages; for our true significance is more than personal, it is bound up with the fact of our status as members of a supernatural society. So into all the affairs of the little house there should enter a certain sense of the city and beyond this of the infinite world in which the city stands: some

11

awestruck memory of our double situation, at once so homely and so mysterious. We must each maintain unimpaired our unique relation with God; yet without forgetting our intimate contact with the rest of the city, or the mesh of invisible life which binds all the inhabitants in one.

For it is on the unchanging Life of God, as on a rock, that the whole city is founded. That august and cherishing Spirit is the atmosphere which bathes it, and fills each room of every little house – quickening, feeding and sustaining. He is the one Reality which makes us real; and, equally, the other houses too. 'If I am not in Thee,' said St Augustine, 'then I am not at all.' We are often urged to think of the spiritual life as a personal adventure, a ceaseless hustle forward; with all its meaning condensed in the 'perfection' of the last stage. But though progress, or rather growth, is truly in it, such growth in so far as it is real can only arise from, and be conditioned by, a far more fundamental relation – the growing soul's abidingness in God.

House Design

Next, what type of house does the soul live in? It is a two-storey house. The psychologist too often assumes that it is a one-roomed cottage with a mud floor; and never even attempts to go upstairs. The extreme transcendentalist sometimes talks as though it were perched in the air, like the lake dwellings of our primitive ancestors, and had no ground floor at all. A more humble attention to facts suggests that neither of these simplifications is true. We know that we have a ground floor, a natural life biologically conditioned, with animal instincts and affinities; and that this life is very important, for it is the product of the divine creativity – its builder and maker is God. But we know too that we have an upper floor, a supernatural life, with supernatural possibilities, a capacity for God; and that this, man's peculiar prerogative, is more important still. If we try to live on one floor alone we destroy the mysterious beauty of our human vocation; so utterly a part of the fugitive and creaturely life of this planet and yet so deeply coloured by Eternity; so entirely one with the world of nature and yet, 'in the Spirit, a habitation of God: Thou madest him lower than the angels, to crown him with glory and worship.' We are created both in Time and in Eternity, not truly one but truly two; and every thought, word and act must be subdued to the dignity of that double situation in which Almighty God has placed and companions the childish spirit of man.

A House for God

Therefore a full and wholesome spiritual life can never consist in living upstairs and forgetting to consider the ground floor and its homely uses and needs; thus ignoring the humbling fact that those upper rooms are entirely supported by it. Nor does it consist in the constant, exasperated investigation of the shortcomings of the basement. When St Teresa said that her prayer had become 'solid like a house' she meant that its foundations now went down into the lowly but firm ground of human nature, the concrete actualities of the natural life: and, on those solid foundations, its walls rose up towards heaven. The strength of the house consisted in that intimate welding together of the divine and the human, which she found in its perfection in the humanity of Christ. There, in the common stuff of human life which He blessed by His presence, the saints have ever seen the homely foundations of holiness. Since we are two-storey creatures, called to a natural and a supernatural status, both sense and spirit must be rightly maintained, kept in order, consecrated to the purposes of the city, if our full obligations are to be fulfilled. The house is built for God; to reflect, on each level, something of His unlimited Perfection. Downstairs that general rightness of adjustment to all this-world obligations, which the ancients called the quality of Justice; and the homely virtues of Prudence, Temperance and Fortitude reminding us of our creatureliness, our limitations, and so humbling and disciplining us. Upstairs, the heavenly powers of Faith, Hope and Charity; tending towards the Eternal, nourishing our life towards God, and having no meaning apart from God.

Care of the Whole House

But the soul's house will never be a real home unless the ground floor is as cared for and as habitable as the beautiful rooms upstairs. We are required to live in the whole of our premises, and are responsible for the condition of the whole of our premises. It is useless to repaper the drawing-room if what we really need is a new sink. In that secret Divine purpose which is drawing all life towards perfection, the whole house is meant to be beautiful and ought to be beautiful; for it comes from God, and was made to His design. Christ's soul when on earth lived in one of these houses; had to use the same fitments, make the same arrangements do. We cannot excuse our own failures by attributing them to the inconvenience of the premises and the fact that some very old-fashioned bits of apparatus survive. Most of us have inherited some ugly bits of furniture, or unfortunate family portraits which we can't get rid of, and which prevent our rooms being quite a success. Nevertheless the soul does not grow strong merely by enjoying its upstairs privileges and ignoring downstairs disadvantages, problems and responsibilities; but only by tackling its real task of total transformation. It is called to maintain a house which shall be in its completeness 'a habitation of God in the Spirit'; subdued to His purpose on all levels, manifesting His glory in what we call spiritual life. For man is the link between these two orders; truly created a little lower than the angels, yet truly crowned with glory and worship, because in this unperfected human nature the Absolute Life itself has deigned to dwell.

The Soul, a House of Prayer

That means, reduced to practice, that the whole house with its manifold and graded activities must be a house of prayer. It does not mean keeping a quiet room to which we can retreat, with mystical pictures on the walls, and curtains over the windows to temper the disconcerting intensity of the light; a room where we can forget the fact that there are black beetles in the kitchen and that the cooker is not working very well. Once we admit any violent contrast between the upper and lower floor, the 'instinctive' and 'spiritual' life, or feel a reluctance to investigate the humbling realities of the basement, our life becomes less, not more, than human; and our position is unsafe. Are we capable of the adventure of courage which inspires the great prayer of St Augustine: 'The house of my soul is narrow; do Thou enter in and enlarge it! It is ruinous; do Thou repair it'? Can we risk the visitation of the mysterious Power that will go through all our untidy rooms, showing up their shortcomings and their possibilities; reproving by the tranquillity of order the waste and muddle of our inner life? The mere hoarded rubbish that ought to go into the dustbin; the things that want mending and washing; the possessions we have never taken the trouble to use? Yet this is the only condition on which man can participate in that fullness of life for which he is made.

The Household Prayer

The Lord's Prayer, in which St Teresa said that she found the whole art of contemplation from its simple beginning to its transcendent goal, witnesses with a wonderful beauty and completeness to this two-storey character of the soul's house; and yet its absolute unity. It begins at the top, in the watch tower of faith, with the sublime assertion of our supernatural status – the one relation, intimate yet inconceivable, that governs all the rest – 'Our Father who art in Heaven, hallowed be Thy name.'

Whatever the downstairs muddle and tension we have to deal with, however great the difficulty of adjusting the claims of the instincts that live in the basement and the interests that clamour at the door, all these demands, all this rich and testing experience, is enfolded and transfused by the cherishing, over-ruling life and power of God. We are lifted clear of the psychological tangle in which the life of our spirit too often seems enmeshed, into the pure, serene light of Eternity; and shown the whole various and disconcerting pageant of creation as proceeding from God, and existing only that it may glorify His name. Childlike dependence and joyful adoration are placed together as the twin characters of the soul's relation to God.

Thence, step by step, this prayer brings us downstairs, goes with us through the whole house; bringing the supernatural into the natural, blessing and sanctifying, cleansing and rectifying every aspect of the home. 'Thy Kingdom come!' Hope – trustful expectation. 'Thy will be done!' Charity – the loving union of our wills with the Infinite Will. Then the ground floor. 'Give us this day' – that food from beyond ourselves which nourishes and sustains our life. Forgive us all our little failures and excesses, neutralise the corroding power of our conflicts, disharmonies, rebellions, sins. We can't deal with them alone. Teach us, as towards our fellow citizens, to share that general tolerance of God. Lead us not into situations where we are tried beyond our strength; but meet us on the battlefield of personality, and protect the weakness of the adolescent spirit against the downward pull of the inhabitants of the lower floor.

And then, the reason of all this; bringing together, in one supreme declaration of joy and confidence, the soul's sense of that supporting, holy and eternal Reality who is the Ruler and the Light of the city, and of every room in every little house. Thine is the Kingdom, the Power and the Glory. If our interior life be subdued to the spirit of this prayer, with its rich sense of our mighty heritage and childlike status, our total dependence on the Reality of God, then the soul's house is truly running well. Its action is transfused by contemplation. The door is open between the upper and the lower floors; the life of spirit and life of sense.

The Two Cities

'Two cities,' said St Augustine, 'have been created by two loves: the earthly city by love of self even to contempt of self. The one city glories in itself; the other city glories in the Lord. The one city glories in its own strength; the other city says to its God, "I will love Thee, O Lord my strength." ' Perhaps there has never been a time in Christian history when that contrast has been more sharply felt than it is now – the contrast between that view of man's situation and meaning, in which the emphasis falls on humanity, its vast desires and wonderful achievements, even to contempt of God; and the view in which the emphasis falls on God's transcendent action and over-ruling will, even to contempt of self. St Augustine saw, and still would see, mankind ever at work building those two cities; and every human soul as a potential citizen of one or the other. And from this point of view, that which we call the 'interior life' is just the home life of those who inhabit the invisible City of God; realistically taking up their municipal privileges and duties, and pursuing them 'even to contempt of self'. It is the obligation and the art of keeping the premises entrusted to us in good order, having ever in view the welfare of the city as a whole.

Gift not Effort

Some souls, like some people, can be slummy anywhere. There is always a raucous and uncontrolled voice ascending from the basement, and a pail of dirty water at the foot of the stairs. Others can achieve in the most impossible situation a simple and beautiful life. The good citizen must be able without reluctance to open the door at all times, not only at the week-end; must

17

keep the windows clean and taps running properly, that the light and living water may come in. These free gifts of the supernatural are offered to each house; and only as free gifts can they be had. Our noisy little engine will not produce the true light; nor our most desperate digging a proper water supply. Recognition of this fact, this entire dependence of the creature, is essential if the full benefits of our mysterious citizenship are ever to be enjoyed by us. 'I saw,' said the poet of the Apocalypse, 'the holy city coming down from God out of heaven . . . the glory of God lit it . . . the water of life proceeded out of the throne of God.' All is the free gift of the supernatural; not the result of human growth and effort. God's generous and life-giving work in the world of souls ever goes before man's work in God. So the main thing about the Invisible City is not the industry and good character of the inhabitants: they do not make it shine. It is the tranquil operation of that perpetual providence, which incites and supports their small activities; the direct and childlike relation in which they stand to the city's Ruler; the generous light and air that bathe the little houses; the unchanging rock of Eternity on which their foundations stand.

Degrees of Prayer

Communion with Spiritual Reality

Every religious mind is, of course, familiar with the idea of prayer; and in one degree or another, with the practice of it. Yet we sometimes forget how very little we really know about it; how personal and subjective are the accounts spiritual writers give of it; how empirical and how obscure in its deepest moments, even for the best of us, our own understanding of it must be. Here we are, little half-animal, half-spiritual creatures, mysteriously urged from within and enticed from without to communion with spiritual reality. If and when we surrender to this craving and this attraction, we enter thereby – though at first but dimly – on a completely new life, full of variety, of new joy, tension and pain, and offering an infinite opportunity of development to us. Such is the life of prayer, as understood by the mystics, and as practised with greater or less completeness of surrender and reward by all real lovers of Christ.

In prayer, we open up our souls to the Divine energy and grace perpetually beating in on us; and receive that energy and grace, in order that it may be transmuted by our living zest into work – may cleanse, invigorate and slowly change us. It is therefore of primary importance to all Christians to know how best to set up and maintain the contacts of prayer. This is a difficult art – we should bring intelligence as well as love to bear on it.

Christian spirituality seeks union with God in order that we may better serve the purposes of His will; and one of the ways in which this is done is by the expansion of the prayerful consciousness. Anything, therefore, which we can find out about this is a true extension of our knowledge of the Kingdom of Heaven.

Prayer: a Devout Intent

The first thing that occurs to us is, that all the machinery of prayer has but one very simple object – our loving intercourse with God – and that all progress in it can be described as an increased closeness in the intercourse and an increased perfection in the love. The varieties and degrees of the machinery have in themselves no intrinsic importance, except in so far as they contribute to this. We study them, as we study the normal development of bodily or mental activity, because we find, in practice, that they occur; and it is better and more healthy to know this, than to be baffled and puzzled when, for instance, we find ourselves for the first time plunged in the prayer of simplicity, and unable to make use of our ordinary forms. But, in considering our own prayer, it is of little importance to ask ourselves whether we have attained this or that degree, but of great importance to ask ourselves what is the condition and attitude of our souls in the degree which we find ourselves to be practising – whether this prayer is truly humbling, bracing, and vivifying us, or merely inducing a state of emotional languor or spiritual strain. All the greatest masters of prayer bring home to us the simple, natural, unforced character of real intercourse with God. They say again and again that prayer is nothing else but a devout intent directed towards Him; and this intent expresses itself in various ways. The beginner must be shown these ways, and often be helped to use them; but in the mature man or woman of prayer their exercise is free and spontaneous. Perhaps there is no other department of the spiritual life in which St Augustine's great saying, 'Love, and do what you like', becomes more completely true. Julian of Norwich says at the end of her Revelations, that what she has found and felt most fully is 'the homeliness, courtesy and naturehood of God'. So the soul's real progress is not towards some mysterious, abnormal and trance-like condition; but rather towards the unspoilt, trustful, unsophisticated apprehension of the little child.

Praying naturally

We cannot by stretching ourselves add an inch to our stature: the result will be strain, not growth. All this means that we should be very chary of taking at face value the advice given in little books about 'going into the silence' and so on: and should never treat this advice as though it were applicable to every soul at every time. Real inward silence is not achieved by any deliberate spiritual trick. It develops naturally; and most often from the full exercise of mental prayer, which is in its turn the child of properly practised vocal prayer. Therefore I think that no one ought to set to work to practise such inward silence until they feel a strong impulse so to do. If we try such artificial methods, we probably drift into a mere quietistic reverie; and such reverie, though pleasant, has nothing in common with real contemplative prayer. So, we shall do best if we enter on the study of the degrees of prayer safeguarded by this principle: that whilst keeping in mind the highest ideal of attainment, we are never to struggle for a degree or condition of fervour in which we do not naturally find ourselves. People are often encouraged to do this by indiscriminate reading of ascetic and mystical literature, a practice to which real dangers are attached. They browse among descriptions and counsels intended only for advanced souls, and struggle to produce states of consciousness far beyond their power. These states will arise within us naturally and simply, only when and if we are ready for them. In all normal cases, God feeds and leads the soul very gently. Growth is gradual. The many adjustments necessary to the full establishment of the prayerful consciousness take time; and often its advance is checked by periods of dullness, fatigue and incapacity which are explicable by psychology, and must be borne with patience as instruments of our purificiation. All the great masters of prayer refer to them, and insist, too, that humble surrender, not constant fervour, is the best index of the soul's good-will. Thus Walter Hilton says: 'When thou disposest thee to think of God, if thy heart be dull and dark, and feels neither wit nor savour nor devotion for to think, but only a bare desire and a weak will that thou shouldst think of God, but thou canst not – then I hope it is good to thee that thou strive not much with thyself, as if thou wouldst by thine own might overcome thyself.' Here Hilton shows himself to be intuitively aware of that which psychologists now call the law of Reversed Effort – the fact that such desperate striving with ourselves merely frustrates its own end, and increases our baffled sense of helplessness. And again, to the soul dissatisfied with its ordinary prayers and hankering after contemplation, he says: 'Press not too much thereafter, as if thou wert abiding or gaping after some strange stirring or some wonderful feeling other than thou hast had.' And another old English mystic tells us not to be like 'greedy greyhounds' snatching at God's gifts, but to come gently and willingly to His outstretched hand and take what He gives us.

Degrees of Prayer

We take, then, as our first principle the humble and diligent use of the degree of prayer natural to a soul at any particular stage of its course, and not the anxious straining towards, some other degree yet beyond it: and as our second principle, that prayer has its psychological, as well as its spiritual side, and in the effort to understand it better we should keep our eye on both. It has been well said that our Lord in all His acts and teaching kept His eye on man as he really is: and here, in particular, we should make a humble but persistent effort to follow Him. From this point we can go on to consider what the degrees of prayer really are. Spiritual writers give them various names and divisions, but as matter of fact they shade into one another, forming, as it were, a sliding scale from the simplest prayer of the Christian child to the infused contemplation of the soul absorbed in God. I propose now to make five divisions, and these are: Vocal Prayer; Mental Prayer; the Prayer of Immediate Acts; the Prayer of Simplicity; and the Prayer of Quiet. Beyond these are the higher degrees of contemplation, which are outside our present scope.

Vocal Prayer

First, then comes *Vocal Prayer*. We all know what this is; but we do not always remember, in our eagerness for something more spiritual, that apart from its devotional aspect, its educative value for the soul that uses it is greater than is sometimes supposed. In vocal prayer we speak, not only to God, but also to ourselves. We are filling our minds with acts of love, praise, humility and penitence, which will serve us well in times when the power of mental prayer seems to fail us and the use of these formulae becomes the only way of turning to God left within our reach. Moreover, psychology insists that the spoken word has more suggestive power, is more likely to reach and modify our deeper psychic levels, than any inarticulate thought; for the centres of speech are closely connected with the heart of our mental life. Therefore those who value the articulate recitation of a daily office, the use of litanies and psalms, are keeping closer to the facts of existence than those who only talk generally of remaining in a state of prayer. I feel sure that some vocal prayer should enter into the daily rule even of the most contemplative soul. It gives shape and discipline to our devotions, and keeps us in touch with the great traditions of the Church. Moreover, such vocal prayers, if we choose them well, have the evocative quality of poetry: they rouse the dormant spiritual sense, and bring us into the presence of God. 'Oft it falls,' says Hilton, 'that praying with thy mouth gets and keeps fervour of devotion, and if a man cease from saying, devotion vanishes away.'

As the life of prayer begins to exert its full power, such vocal prayers will gradually but steadily become slower and more pondered. The soul finds in their phrases more and more significance, makes of these phrases special applications, and is led on by them to petitions and aspirations of its own. This means that it is drawing near to the next stage, that of meditation. This is the first degree of mental prayer; that is to say, prayer in which we do not repeat set forms, but do something on our own account. Meditation is a word which covers a considerable range of devotional states. It is perhaps most simply defined as thinking in the Presence of God. And since our ordinary thoughts are scattered, seldom poised for long on one point, but evoked and influenced by a multitude of external things, real meditation requires as its preliminary what ascetic writers call recollection – a deliberate gathering of ourselves together, a retreat into our own souls. This is more easily done by a simple exercise of the imagination, a gentle turning to God, than by those ferocious efforts towards concentrating which some manuals on prayer advise, and which often end by concentrating attention on the concentration itself. I will not go further into their technical descriptions of method, which seem so difficult when we read them, and often worry people needlessly. There is no virtue in any one method, except in so far as it succeeds; and different methods succeed with different souls. For some, the slow reading of a passage in the Bible or *The Imitation of Christ* leads directly to a state of prayer; for others, a quiet dwelling on one of God's attributes is a gateway to adoration. Articulate speech is now left aside, but the ceaseless stream of inward discourse may persist, and become a secret conversation with God; while others will be led to consideration, a quiet ruminating on spiritual things. Every real meditation involves three points: we think in some way of the subject of our meditation; we feel the emotion, whether of love, penitence or joy, which it suggests to us; and finally, the aim of all meditative prayer is a resolution, or a renewal of our surrender to God – this is an act of the will.

Varieties of Meditations

Practically every person who prays at all, and has not reached one of the stages of contemplative prayer, can meditate in a simple way if he chooses to practise this art; and it is most fruitful, especially perhaps in the early stages of the spiritual life, whilst the purgation and remaking of character is still in the foreground. It comes naturally to people of active minds, the reasoners, and the ponderers; who have only to occupy their normal thinking powers on spiritual material for a set period of each day in order to develop it. Many souls remain in this type of prayer throughout their spiritual course. Within its own limitations it gives ample scope for variety; and this is a great need if the life of prayer is to be kept in a wholesome state. It can be applied to a wide range of subjects and conditions of the soul; extending from the simplest reflections, considerations and talkings to God, arising often out of our reading or our vocal or liturgical prayer, to the beginnings of those spontaneous acts of the will and heart which are really the first movements towards the next degree of prayer; that is to say, the *Prayer of Immediate Acts*.

Prayer of Immediate Acts

The transition from meditation to immediate acts takes place only in those souls which have some tendency to contemplation; not perhaps much, but still an aptitude seeking expression. By them it is commonly felt as a decreasing inclination to reason or discourse in prayer, and an increasing inclination to simple, spontaneous expressions of love and penitence. It is true that the praying self does think; but not with the same method and completeness as before. It now dwells more and more on the affections; on acts of love and adoration, meek aspirations to God, expressed in short phrases which may seem banal enough when we read them in books of devotion, but become charged, for the soul in this degree, with the most intense significance. We remember the favourite aspiration of St Francis: 'My God, my God, what art Thou and what am I?' Such aspirations, formed from memories of past reading and prayers, rise spontaneously into consciousness as the prayer proceeds; and those whose minds are richly stored with Scripture phrases and liturgical forms will seldom be at a loss for them. They are, however, only the expression of the act. 'Press thou towards God with the sharp dart of thy longing love,' says the author of *The Cloud of Unknowing* in his directions for this prayer, 'and take no thought for words.' Intuition here begins to take the place of logical considerations; and, as psychologists would say, affective thought as well as rational thought is taken up into the life of prayer, which now overflows its first boundaries and invades wider and wider regions of the self. As this degree matures in those to whom it is appropriate, the 'immediate acts' of the heart decrease and will grow simpler and rarer. There is often a marked distaste and inability for meditation. There are pauses, periods of deep silence, hushed communion which the soul feels to be more and more fruitful. Here we are at the threshold of that progressive absorption which leads to the true contemplative state.

Prayer of Simplicity

Gradually one act of will, affection or aspiration comes more and more to dominate the whole prayer, say of half an hour's duration or more: and is used merely to true up that state of attention which is the very heart of prayer. When this condition is established, the soul has reached the degree which is sometimes called the *Prayer of Simplicity*, and sometimes that of repose, simple attention or active contemplation. It is thrown open with great love and desire to God, but in so simple a way that it cannot analyse its own experience. Its whole impulse is to wait on Him rather than to speak to Him. It was in the effort to describe the

26

apprehensions of this degree that the author of *The Cloud of Unknowing* said, 'God may well be loved, but not thought. Therefore, I will leave all I can think and take to my love that which I cannot think.' Nevertheless I am sure it is a mistake to imagine that such prayer can be well developed and preserved, unless a certain care be given to its mental preparation. It is far better to enter it with *some* idea or disposition in the mind, some special thought of God, some distinct orientation of the will, than in the state of vague blankness characteristic of quietism; for this will merely encourage distraction and religious day-dreams, and may even bring about a sort of self-hypnotisation. The ultimate object of all prayer is greater efficiency for God, not the limp self-abandonment of quietism; and therefore as the soul approaches the passive degrees a careful discrimination becomes necessary. The direction of the mystics is that we should enter on simple contemplation with 'a devout intent directed to God', and there is something very definite about that.

Contemplation

We often confuse ourselves by speaking and thinking of contemplation as a 'state'. It is not a state in the sense of being static, a continuous unchanging condition. In all those degrees of prayer which we are considering, a constant variety of acts is normal, wholesome and inevitable. Though a rapt attention to God dominates the prayer, within this attention must fluctuate, thoughts and acts must arise from time to time. To say this is only to say that our mental life persists in it. Now when these thoughts and acts, these ripples on the deep pool of contemplation, are born of that profound feeling of charity and compassion which cannot long remain untouched by our neighbours' needs and griefs, then surely intercession of the very best kind is exercised by us. For intercession is a special and deliberate way of exercising love, in completest union with the Love of God. And to be in perfect charity with all men is already to intercede for them; to put, as it were, our spiritual weight on their side of the scale.

These four degrees of prayer – that is, ordinary vocal prayer, mental prayer or meditation, immediate acts and simplicity – are to a great extent within the self's control. In theological language they are natural and not supernatural degrees. Once they are thoroughly established, the soul can normally and under suitable conditions produce them. But with the real *Prayer of Quiet*, we pass beyond this condition. It is wholly involuntary. None can produce it of themselves; and it seems always to come as a distinct and irresistible experience from without. In technical terms, it is 'infused' or the work of grace. In this real quiet, which may come suddenly upon the soul in the course of its ordinary prayer, it is not merely drawn towards a simple and imageless attention to God and aspiration towards Him. It is more or less intensely aware of His Presence. Here in fact, we have the first faint emergence of mystical consciousness, in stillness and humility receiving the obscure impression of the Divine. In the prayer of simplicity and aspiration, the deeps of the unconscious are opened up to God; and that this is veritably done in these degrees is proved by their effect on the impulsive sources of conduct. But in the quiet, and the simple union which is the full development of quiet, this apprehension overflows into consciousness; and this is something which the self cannot effect by the exercise of will. All great writers on prayer insist on this point.

Sometimes the establishment of this new degree comes by way of a painful inward struggle and aridity; what St John of the Cross has described as 'the night of the senses' – a period of distress and obscurity, in which it seems to the soul that it is losing all it had gained of the life of prayer. This is more especially felt by people who have real contemplative aptitude, and whom this type of spirituality is destined in the end to dominate. It meets and must conquer many resistances in their active minds, must cut for itself new paths; and this may involve tension and suffering and the apparent withdrawal of the ordinary power of prayer. Here is a point at which skilled and sympathetic guidance is of special service to the soul, which is often bewildered and disheartened by its own experience, its strange sense of dimness and incapacity. Others, whose natural level is, and may always remain the prayer of aspiration or of simplicty, may find themselves plunged in the quiet from time to time; and will obtain from this experience a refreshment, power and absolute certitude which the other degrees of prayer cannot give.

Beyond the Degrees

Beyond this point it is hardly I think for us, as ordinary Christians, to explore; and indeed the cold analysis of these living experiences can only be justified by a longing to help other souls on the path which leads to closer knowledge of God. There is real truth in Hilton's warning that 'a ransacker of the might of God and His Majesty, without great purity and meekness, shall be overlaid and oppressed of himself'. And perhaps nothing could be worse for our devotional life than perpetual exploration of that which lies far beyond us. But, looking back at the degrees which we have considered, there are two points regarding them which it is well that we should bear in mind. The first is of practical, the second of psychological interest.

The practical point is this. The use of the higher degrees of prayer does not and should not ever mean the total abandonment of the lower degrees. The soul adds on new ways of intercourse; but this does not involve the abolishing of the old ways – that because she has reached the quiet joy of simplicity she is never to use formal prayer, never to discourse or think out her ideas before God, or make deliberate acts of penitence and love. To suppose this is the fundamental error of quietism. The healthiness of our spiritual life, like that of our mental life, depends to a great extent on its suppleness, and on the variety which we are able to impart to it. We should never, therefore, be afraid of such variety, or suppose we are losing ground if we find ourselves again using discursive prayer or formal acts after practising the higher degrees. The mystics are insistent on this point. Thus St John of the Cross says, that when the soul is not in the prayer of simplicity it 'ought to avail itself in all its exercises of the help of good thoughts and meditations, according to what brings it the greatest spiritual profit'. And St Teresa still more strongly – 'Since God has given the powers of the soul in order that we may use them, and the work of each has its reward, instead of trying to imprison them by a sort of enchantment let them freely perform their ordinary office, until it pleases God to raise them to a higher state.'

It is, therefore, best to be ready to go up and down the ladder of love: sometimes speaking and sometimes listening, sometimes thinking and sometimes resting in the communion which is beyond thought and speech. A quiet and meek retreat to a lower degree of prayer, which one can do, is worth far more than the anxious struggle to tune oneself up to a degree which (anyhow for the moment) one cannot do. Self-will in prayer is a subtle temptation, known to most religious people. But there is always some way of turning to God which is within our reach, however distracted or weary we may be: and as a general rule, it is surely better to begin there, quite simply, though the crudity and childishness of our level of feeling and expression may deal a smart blow at our self-respect. Constituted as we are, it is inevitable that our spiritual aptitude should fluctuate, as does the rest of our plastic and unstable psychic life. This limitation ought not to depress us, but it ought to keep us in humility; and humility is the one grace which gives wings to the simplest prayer.

Intercession

The Mystery of Intercession

Consider for a moment what is implied in the amazing mystery of intercession; at least in the little that we understand of it. It implies first our implicit realisation of God, the infinitely loving, living and all-penetrating Spirit of Spirits, as an Ocean in which we all are bathed. And next, speaking still that spatial language to which our human thinking is tied down, that somehow through this uniting and vivifying medium we too, being one with Him in love and will, can mutually penetrate, move and influence each other's souls in ways as yet unguessed; yet throughout the whole process moulded and determined by the prevenient, personal, free and everpresent God. The world He has been and is creating is a world infused through and through with Spirit; and it is partly through the prayerful and God-inspired action of men that the spiritual work of this world is done. When a man or woman of prayer, through their devoted concentration, reaches a soul in temptation and rescues it, we must surely acknowledge that this is the action of God Himself, using that person as an instrument.

Redeeming Prayer

In this mysterious interaction of energies it seems that one tool is put into our hands: our love, will, interest, desire – four words describing four aspects of one thing. This dynamic love, once purged of self-interest, is ours to use on spiritual levels; it is an engine for working with God on other souls. The saints so used it, often at tremendous cost to themselves, and with tremendous effect. As their personality grew in strength and expanded in adoration, so they were drawn on to desperate and heroic wresting for souls; to those exhausting and creative activities, that steady and generous giving of support, that redeeming prayer by which human spirits are called to work with God. Especially in its most mysterious reaches, in its redemptive, self-immolating action on suffering and sin, their intercession dimly reproduces and continues the supernatural work of Christ. Real saints do feel and bear the weight of the sins and pains of the world. It is the human soul's greatest privilege that we can thus accept redemptive suffering for one another – and they do.

The Work of Love

'God *enabled* me to agonise in prayer,' said the saintly evangelical, David Brainerd. 'My soul was drawn out very much for the world. I grasped for a multitude of souls.' Does not that give to us a sense of unreached possibilities, of deep mysterious energies; something not quite covered by what are usually called 'intercessions'? So too St Teresa says that if anyone claiming to be united to God is always in a state of peaceful beatitude, she simply does not believe in their union with God. Such a union, to her mind, involves great sorrow for the sin and pain of the world; a sense of identity not only with God but also with other souls, and a great longing to redeem and heal. That is real supernatural charity. It is a call to love and save not the nice but the nasty; not the lovable but the unlovely, the hard, the narrow, and the embittered, and the tiresome, who are so much worse. To love irrespective of merit or opinion or personal preference; to love even those who offend our taste. If you are to love people thus, translating your love, as you must, into unremitting intercessory work, and avoid being swamped by the great ocean of suffering, sin and need to which you are sent;

32

once again this will only be done by maintaining and feeding the temper of adoration and trustful adherence. This is the heart of the life of prayer; and only in so far as we work from this centre can we safely dare to touch other souls and seek to affect them. For such intercession is a sacrifical job; and sacrificial jobs need the support of a strong inner life if they are to be carried through. They are rooted and grounded in love.

Meditation

A Meditation is not itself a Prayer. It is a sort of technique which leads to prayer, turns our minds and hearts and wills towards God, and so helps our communion with Him. When the actual meditation, the considering and applying of the subject, has led us into prayer, it has done all it is wanted to do – we can let it drop away and continue quite simply our converse with God and self-offering to God.

The Rich Young Man

The picture we are going to look at now is that of the young man who came to our Lord and said, 'What shall I do to inherit eternal life?' In other words, 'How shall I make my life *real*?'

And first we kneel in silence and ask God to show us in this meditation that which He wants us to learn, and to open our minds to His Light.

The Gospel of Mark (chapter 10 verses 17 – 22).
And when he was gone forth into the way, there came one running, and kneeled to him, and asked him, Good Master, what shall I do that I may inherit eternal life?

And Jesus said unto him, Why callest thou me good? there is none good but one, that is God. Thou knowest the commandments, Do not commit adultery, Do not kill, Do not steal, Do not bear false witness, Defraud not, Honour thy father and thy Mother.

And he answered and said unto him, Master, all these have I observed from my youth. Then Jesus, beholding him loved him and said unto him, One thing thou lackest: go thy way, sell whatsoever thou hast, and give to the poor, and thou shalt have treasure in heaven: and come, take up the cross, and follow me. And he was sad at that saying and went away grieved: for he had great possessions.

Look well at this picture. Enter into it. Make yourselves part of it. Use your imagination freely. Consider that what is said is said to you and what is here shown is shown to you. Where are you and what do you see? You are in Palestine, among the little group trying to follow Christ and learn from Him. You see Him as He moves quietly about the country, exercising His strange attractive power, as He exercises it still – even on those who do not want to surrender to Him. The attraction of the Light of the World, of the One who has the words of Eternal Life which everyone really longs to hear, never forcing His demands but drawing people like a magnet, by the power of pure self-forgetful love.

And then we see the young man.

Virtuous, prosperous, what we should call quite the best type, with good traditions, a good background. And yet, somehow, dissatisfied. He has felt the attraction, recognised one who can give the only final answer to his problem, and comes running – with that rush with which we respond to real beauty, real goodness, real light – and kneels to that revelation of all he longs for and needs to know – as we kneel now. And he asks Jesus what is the price of full life: life in God and for God.

And our Lord quotes him two prices. He quotes first the price of a respectable piety, being a good Christian, a good Churchman. The young man has paid that, but somehow it has not brought what he wanted. And then, looking at him with love and so desiring for him the full joy of his supernatural inheritance, Jesus quotes him the price of friendship with God – an unreserved consecration, total self-abandonment. Keep the commandments. Follow Me!

Spirit of Jesus! enlighten my eyes as I dwell with you in

the silence, that I may see this choice, the choice which is YOU. And turn my seeing into loving.

Where is that scene staged? In my soul.

When?

Every time I am given a real chance of sacrifice. 'If you would be perfect,' says Christ, 'Be complete: enter My order, stand by Me, leave all possessiveness, all crutches – personal, intellectual, spiritual crutches – all self-interest, self-love, all the things you think you simply must have. Let comfort, popularity, status, appreciation, even affection, come and go as they will; and so achieve My liberty, My timeless joy.'

In spite of appearances to the contrary, one thing only is needful: the same lesson Martha heard with such astonishment. Only a deep and very humble love can recognise *that* truth. Show me what the attachments and cravings are, which hold me down below your level of total self-surrender, real love. Show me the things that lumber up my heart, so that it cannot be filled with Your life and power.

What are they? People? Ambitions? Interests? Comforts? Anxieties? Self-chosen aims?

You know! Show them to me. I come back and kneel at Your feet and look at the wounds on those feet and say again, What shall I do? Give me some of your courage that I may accept the answer, whatever it may be or whatever it costs. For I know that there *is* an answer. I long to be complete in Your service, transmit Your love, live in Your order.

Take from me all that hinders and teach me to accept in its place all that you accept; the ceaseless demands, needs, conflicts, pressures, misunderstandings even of those who loved You best.

Help me to discern the particular price you ask and help me to pay the particular price – whatever it may be.

Perhaps You have taken away from me the joy of communion with You, that once I had: perhaps You ask me to walk for a time without Your felt presence, in poverty of spirit. You sent the seventy disciples away from You to do Your will. They went

36

without question and they returned with joy. So may it be with me.

Perhaps You have given me the holy privilege or opportunity of serving Your poor, as Your representative on earth.

Cleanse my service of all selfishness, spiritual or material, all criticism or impatience, all secret desire for consolation, recognition or reward.

All that seems pretty mean, as I kneel at your feet. Help me to remember that undemanding service is Your standard. The first shall be last and the last shall be first with You.

Let me be content to follow You in anxiety, failure, weariness, darkness, loneliness and contempt.

Let me be content to follow You up to Calvary.

It is the only path: the way to Eternal Life. But I cannot climb that hill unless I leave my luggage behind. The straight way goes through Gethsemane.

Have I enough courage for that? You did not save the world by Your wonderful teachings or even by Your works of mercy. You saved it by utter self-giving, courage and love: the Cross. Turn my seeing into loving.

Perhaps You have given me a tiny share in Your teaching, hearing, saving or rescuing work: some place on Your staff.

May I love those You have given me, to the end, for You and in Your way.

May I give and go on giving.

May I bear and go on bearing.

May I be Your friend, Your servant, Your fellow-worker: one of the myriad channels through which Your Divine Charity flows out without hindrance to the world.

Take all that I have and all that I am and subdue it to Your service.

For this alone is eternal Life.

Read:

Thomas à Kempis
The Imitation of Christ IV, 8

O MASTER CHRIST! Thou has loved us with an everlasting love:

Thou hast forgiven us, trained us, disciplined us:

Thou has broken us loose and laid Thy commandments upon us,

Thou hast set us in the thick of things and deigned to use us:

Thou hast shewn Thyself to us, fed us, guided us:

Be graciously pleased to accept and forgive our efforts

And keep us Thy free bondslaves for ever. Amen.

Emmaus

Let us ask for Our Lord's presence with us:

O BLESSED JESU CHRIST, who didst bid all who carry heavy burdens to come to Thee, refresh us with Thy Presence and Thy Power. Quiet our understandings and give ease to our hearts, by bringing us close to things Infinite and Eternal. Open to us the mind of God, that in His light we may see light. And crown Thy choice of us to be Thy servants, by making us springs of strength and joy to all whom we serve.

The Gospel of Luke (chapter 24 verses 13–30)
And, behold, two of them went that same day to a village called Emmaus, which was from Jerusalem about three score furlongs. And they talked together . . . and reasoned, Jesus himself drew near, and went with them. But their eyes were holden that they should not know him . . .

Lord! Open our eyes that we may behold Thee! Open our ears that they may recognise Thy voice. Not in some special religious experience, some great moment or wonderful service or perfect setting, but just as we go along the common road.

Teach us to recognise and welcome You in ordinary, homely events, for it is there that we shall surely find You.

Emmanuel – God with us! *I am with Thee*, saith the Lord. Help me to remember that, up hill and down dale, in fog and rain and storm.

While they communed and reasoned together, Jesus Himself drew near and went with them. But their eyes were holden that they should not know him.

Lord! has it ever been thus with me? Have I been so busied with my own complexity, that I missed You in your simplicity? So fixed on my preconceived ideas about You, that I did not recognise You where You are? Have talk and arguments absorbed my attention and drowned your voice? Have I gone on worrying about religious problems and difficulties, whilst You, transcending all problems and difficulties, quietly kept pace with me on the road?

And presently Christ enters the conversation and says, 'What is it that you are trying to "talk out" and "get straight", to "think through"?'

And we, still so absorbed in our difficulties and notions, our own point of view, we say:

'What? Where on earth have you been, that you don't recognise the appalling state of the world – and the failure of religion – and the problems that confront us – and how hopeless it all looks just now for religious people like us who thought God would intervene and save His people. Things are specially difficult and puzzling for Christians at this moment, and we are having a conference about it, getting more and more confused as we go on.'

Lord! We are often daunted and puzzled, lost in the clash of events and hopes and doubts, disappointments and explanations – too full of prejudice, confused by our own ideas, looking for something large and showy: and so we lose the chance of all You

39

have to give to those who live by prayer and walk with you. Come and walk by us. Our eyes are holden. We have not got the clue to history. You have the clue.

And then *You* speak – 'O slow of heart' – not slow of head; slow of heart, unloving – 'not to see that it had to be like this if love is All!' And You explain to us the mysterious scroll of human destiny, with all its pain, violence and darkness, never more mysterious than it is just now; its beauty and nobility, cruelty and injustice – expounding it in the light of God. It all looks different then. And our minds are quietened and humbled and our hearts burn with a strange ardour and longing we do not understand.

We have reached another stage now. We see that life has meaning only in so far as God is in it: and even its most difficult bits have meaning then.

> *Thus it is written, and thus it behoved Christ to suffer, and to rise from the dead the third day: And that repentance and remission of sins should be preached in his name unto all nations, beginning at Jerusalem.*

Bitter suffering, treachery, cruelty, mockery, despair; the clash with Roman tyranny and ecclesiastical malice – out of all that anguish and conflict, Your saving, radiant spirit of love and sacrifice must come. Your prophets always knew it.

But we are so slow to give up our preconceived ideas; our conventional notions, our feeling that everything ought to go smoothly. Come! teach us Your mysterious method, the method of holiness, and give us the docility that can be taught.

The appearance of things often looks very dreadful and hopeless. Injustice and cruelty seem to triumph over goodness. But in and through them, You are walking still, interpreting the scriptures and the things that concern You, in ways we did not expect.

Teach us to stop arguing and listen to Your voice: to be simple and quiet, to accept even when we do not understand, or when Your deep and gentle teaching comes into conflict with our deepest

40

prejudice, our longing for comfort, our hard and fast beliefs.

Come to us with Your living touch on events; Your sacred hand opening the Scriptures. You have the words of Eternal Life.

But that is not enough, is it, for Your full revelation? and our full surrender, certitude, delight. That way we may receive Your teaching, but we cannot recognise Your presence and it is Your Presence that we need.

And they drew nigh unto the village, whither they went: and he made as though he would have gone further. But they constrained him saying, Abide with us: for it is toward evening, and the day is far spent. And he went in to tarry with them.

Not when You stand by us as an explanation of life, but when You enter our life with all its homely limitations, as Friend and Guest. Come in to abide with us, accepting what we have to offer; when the mysterious pilgrim passing through the world who always seems to be going further than we are, towards a strange, unknown destination – turns a chance meeting into something far deeper and closer, something we can never describe and never forget.

But that will not happen unless I ask You for it, unless I open the door. Only my desire, constraining You will make you come in, abide with me, share my small premises, my humble life. The choice is left to me.

Lord! Give me courage and love to open the door and constrain You to enter, offer all my resources, whatever the disguise You come in, even before I fully recognise my guest.

Come in! Enter my small life!

Lay Your sacred hands on all the common things and small interests of that life and bless and change them. Transfigure my small resources, make them sacred. And in them give me Your very Self.

When out of the heart of my own homely circumstances, You feed me – then my eyes are open to the Presence I long for and can never understand.

LORD! going out from this silence, teach me to be more alert, humble, expectant, than I have been in the past: ever ready to encounter You in quiet, homely ways: in every appeal to my compassion, every act of unselfish love which shows up and humbles my imperfect love, may I recognise You: still walking through the world. Give me that grace of simplicity which alone can receive Your mystery.

Come and abide with me!

Meet me, walk with me!

Enlighten my mind!

And then, Come in! Enter my humble life with its poverty and its limitations as You entered the stable of Bethlehem, the workshop of Nazareth, the cottage of Emmaus.

Bless and consecrate the material of that small and ordinary life.

Feed and possess my soul.

Prayers

And now we go on to another point. I am to think of my small, formless, imperfect soul as constantly subject to the loving, creative action of God, here and now, in all the bustle of my daily life, its ups and downs, its anxieties and tensions and its dreary, unspiritual stretches – and gradually giving it, through these things, its ordained form and significance.

So all the events of my life, even the most trivial events, are ways in which I experience His presence. I might review my life in the stillness, from this point of view, and so deepen my gratitude and awe.

In every person who enters my life, every joy, or grief, or sacrifice, or temptation, or opportunity, or relationship – I feel the delicate touch of God, the action of a living, personal Reality.

And so my true life consists, not in self-development or self-chosen achievement – not in that ceaseless conflict of impulse and reaction which makes my surface so unquiet, but in an ever increasing correspondence with His Life, a loving, humble, recognition and acceptance of the Spirit's action – especially when it thwarts my best intentions and actions and changes the shape of the creature I thought I was going to be.

What has all this to do with my prayer?

Everything.

In prayer my soul and God draw near one another – His fullness to my emptiness. Then, if ever, I realise a little of His patient, brooding action and what His Spirit is working in my deeps. Then His action is most directly felt. So, all my prayer must be penetrated by this sense of my own imperfection and helplessness – this quiet abandonment of my formless soul to the

Spirit that broods on the waters and will bring order into chaos, light into darkness, if I yield myself to His action without reserve.

Without God's grace I am chaos. With His grace I am a tiny bit of the Spiritual World which is being organised for His service.

Come! Creator Spirit! Visiting the minds of Thy people. Fill with grace from above the hearts which Thou has created.

So, what matters most in my prayer is not my desires and feelings, my asking and efforts – not even my poor little bit of worship: but God, Who calls forth these movements in the waters, these stirrings of life.

God, The Master of the Tides, subduing all to His great attraction, His simple aim.

Changing and creating me, bringing out of my very unpromising depths, the surprises of His wisdom and His love: because my tiny will has made a slight response to His Mighty Will.

Thou has fashioned me behind and before and laid Thy hands on me. O let my soul live and it shall praise Thee!

O LORD CHRIST! Who in this difficult world wast tempted in all things like as we are, yet fell into no sin, look pitifully we pray Thee, upon us. Guide us with Thy adorable wisdom. Teach us in every thing and in every hour what we ought to do. Thou alone knowest all our life. Thou alone knowest both what we suffer and what we need. To thee that perfect path which we should walk in, is known. Show it to us and teach us how to walk in it.

Keep us, O Saviour, in body, mind and spirit, for into Thy strong and gentle hands, we commit ourselves . . .

GIVE US LIGHT, O LORD, that contemplating the love and patience of Jesus and His Saints, we may be changed into love and patience.

Take from us by the contemplation of their example, all selfishness. Take from us all softness.

Take from us all delicacy and fastidiousness. Take from us all cowardice and timidity. Take from us all self-love.

Give us a share in their spirit of endurance.

Give us a love of labour.

Give us a love of the Cross.

Give us a love of hardship.

Give us a spirit of courage.

Give us a spirit of surrendered trust.

That we may be willing to spend ourselves and to be spent, for the sake of Thy children, in union with Thy self-giving love.

Sources

'The House of Prayer' comes from *The House of the Soul* (Methuen, 1929).

'Degrees of Prayer' comes from Papers published by the Guild of Health in 1922.

The two meditations were conducted by Evelyn Underhill at Pleshey and published with others in *Meditations and Prayers*.